Malala Yousafzai

Shot by the Taliban, Still Fighting for Equal Education

Malala Yousafzai
Shot by the Taliban, Still Fighting for Equal Education

MATT DOEDEN

LERNER PUBLICATIONS COMPANY • MINNEAPOLIS

Lerner Publications Company
A division of Lerner Publishing Group, Inc.
241 First Avenue North
Minneapolis, MN USA 55401

For reading levels and more information, look up this title at www.lernerbooks.com.

The images in this book are used with the permission of: © Rob Kim/Getty Images, p. 2; © Andrew Burton//Getty Images, p. 6; © pavalena/Shutterstock.com, p. 9; © Veronique de Viguerie/agency/Getty Images, p. 10, 11, 18; © AFP/Stringer/Getty Images, p. 12, 28, 35 (top); © David Allocca/Getty Images, p. 13; © A Majeed/Stringer/Getty Images, p. 15; © Jacques Demarthon/Getty Images, p. 17; AP Photo/Anja Niederinghaus, p. 20; © Todd Strand/ Independent Picture Service, p. 22; © Aamir Qureshi/Getty Images, p. 27, 37 (top); © Stan Honda/ Getty Images, p. 29, 38; © Oli Scarff/Getty Images, p. 30; © Getty Images, p. 35 (bottom); © Robert Nickelsberg/Hulton Archive/Getty Images, p. 39; © Thomas Lohnes/Stringer/Getty Images, p. 40; © The White House/Getty Images, p. 41.

Front Cover: © Christopher Furlong/Getty Images.

Main body text set in Rotis Serif Std 55 Regular 13.5/17. Typeface provided by Adobe Systems.

Library of Congress Cataloging-in-Publication Data

Malala Yousafzai : shot by the Taliban, still fighting for equal education / by Matt Doeden.
    pages   cm. — (Gateway biographies)
Includes index.
ISBN 978–1–4677–4907–7 (lib. bdg. : alk. paper)
ISBN 978–1–4677–4908–4 (eBook)
    1. Yousafzai, Malala, 1997-–Juvenile literature. 2. Girls–Education–Pakistan–Juvenile literature. 3. Girls–Violence against–Pakistan–Juvenile literature. 4. Women social reformers–Pakistan–Biography–Juvenile literature. 5. Taliban–Juvenile literature. 6. Pakistan–Social conditions–Juvenile literature. I. Title.
LC2330.D64 2015
371.822095491–dc23   2013048985

Manufactured in the United States of America
1 – DP – 7/15/14

CONTENTS

Malala Yousafzai advocates for girls' education at the United Nations Youth Assembly on July 12, 2013, in New York City.

October 9, 2012, began much like any other day in Mingora, Pakistan. Fifteen-year-old Malala Yousafzai had just finished a long morning at school. She and her schoolmates—all girls—climbed aboard a bus to go home.

The other girls on the bus wrapped their faces in the tradition of Islam, Pakistan's main religion. But Malala did not wrap hers. She didn't think that she should have to hide her face. For some girls her age, that may have seemed like a very bold stance. But not for Malala. She was used to standing up for what she believed in.

In Pakistan most girls receive little education. Some people, including members of an extreme Islamic group called the Taliban, don't believe girls should go to school at all. But Malala had made herself famous by speaking out for her rights to an education. She and her father, Ziauddin, were among the leaders in a movement to make sure all girls in Pakistan had a chance to go to school.

Malala knew that the Taliban didn't like it when people spoke out against their ideas. Members of the group often attacked people who spoke in ways the Taliban didn't like. Still, Malala never thought the Taliban would attack a teenage girl.

Malala and her schoolmates sang together as the bus rumbled down a rough road. Then the bus came to a sudden stop. Malala watched as a man climbed aboard and began to argue with the bus driver. As they spoke, another man entered the bus from the rear. Most of his face was covered with a handkerchief.

"Who is Malala?" he asked.

No one answered. But some of the girls looked at Malala. That was all the man needed. He pulled out a handgun and pointed it at Malala. The bus erupted in screams. Malala squeezed the hand of her best friend, Moniba. It was her last memory of that day.

The gunman's hands shook as he pulled the trigger three times. The first shot glanced off her head, then traveled into her neck and shoulder. The next two shots hit girls sitting near Malala. Both were hurt, but neither girl died.

The bus driver realized that Malala's injuries were grave. He knew she needed immediate medical attention. He rushed her to the hospital. She was in critical condition. For a time, it looked as though she would die. But she recovered. The Taliban assassin had failed—and Malala's voice for equality was about to grow a whole lot louder.

Child of Pakistan

Malala Yousafzai was born on July 12, 1997, in Mingora, Pakistan. Mingora is the largest city in the Swat District (often called simply Swat, or the Swat Valley) of northern Pakistan. Malala was the first surviving child of her parents, Ziauddin and Tor Pekai. Two sons, Khushal Khan and Atal Khan, joined the family after Malala.

The Yousafzai family is part of the Pashtun ethnic group. Pashtun people come mainly from Afghanistan and Pakistan, which share a border. Traditionally, Pashtun parents value sons much more than daughters. Many feel great disappointment when a baby girl is born. But Ziauddin, a poet and educator, did not feel this way. He was thrilled to have a daughter. And he vowed to give her every opportunity to succeed.

Malala grew up in Mingora, the largest city in the Swat District of Pakistan.

Ziauddin chose Malala's name. He named her after Malalai of Maiwand. Legend tells that this Pashtun girl inspired an Afghan army to defeat British forces in an 1880 battle. It seems that from the beginning, Ziauddin expected big things for his daughter.

When she was born, Malala's parents had little money. Their home had no kitchen, running water, or stove. They couldn't even afford to bring Tor Pekai to a hospital to give birth. Instead, a neighbor came over to deliver the baby girl.

Around this time, Ziauddin and a friend were trying to start a school for girls. The family soon moved into the school building. Little Malala would run around the school, letting herself into classes and even sitting on teachers' laps during class. The idea of girls being educated

At the age of twelve, Malala wanted to become a politician.

Malala grew up in a school for girls that her father ran.

may have seemed strange or wrong to many of the people in her country. But for Malala, school was an important part of everyday life.

"I used to sit in wonder, listening to everything they were being taught," Malala later wrote in her autobiography, *I Am Malala*. "Sometimes I would mimic the teachers. You could say I grew up in a school."

Ziauddin's school became a success. He opened more of them. Malala's family finally had some money. They moved into an apartment. They weren't rich, but Malala and her brothers had everything they needed. Malala remembers her mother sharing food with the poor. She told Malala that she did it because she remembered what it was like to be hungry.

Malala, like her parents, was a devoted Muslim. But she quickly discovered that there were things she didn't like about the Islamic tradition as it was observed in her part of the world. One of them was the way Muslim women were seen as inferior to men. Wives were supposed to obey their husbands. A husband could beat his wife and not suffer any consequences. Girls and women couldn't even go out in public without a male along. And women were expected to cover up thoroughly while in public.

"I had decided very early I would not be like that," Malala later wrote. "But . . . I wondered how free a daughter could ever be."

Girls who live in Islamic nations traditionally cover their faces while in public.

 Changed Region

Life in northern Pakistan was mostly peaceful during the early years of Malala's life. But on September 11, 2001, all that began to change. On that day, members of a terrorist group called al-Qaeda hijacked airplanes. They flew the planes into the World Trade Center in New York City and the Pentagon near Washington, DC, and hijacked another plane that crashed in Pennsylvania.

Smoke billows from the World Trade Center towers after terrorists attacked them on September 11, 2001.

Four-year-old Malala heard the news while at school. But she didn't really understand what was happening. "I had no idea what New York and America were," she later wrote. "The school was my world and my world was the school. We did not realize then that [the attacks] would change our world."

The al-Qaeda terrorists had been closely tied to the Taliban. At the time, the Taliban ruled the nation of Afghanistan. The United States and other nations soon declared war on the Taliban. Afghanistan became a war zone. Many members of the Taliban fled into remote regions of Pakistan—including Swat. They brought their extreme views with them.

Officially, Pakistan sided with the Americans. But secretly, many of its people supported the Taliban. Malala didn't know what to think. She believed that attacking innocent people was wrong. And she resented the Taliban's views on women. But she also didn't think it was right for US troops to invade Afghanistan. Like many Pakistanis, she was torn.

As the war dragged on, many people in Swat began to adopt an even more traditional Islamic stance. In 2004 some of them demanded that Ziauddin shut down his school for girls. But Ziauddin never changed his views or backed down. He refused to close the school. After all, his daughter was one of its brightest students. The seven-year-old was at the top of her class. Ziauddin wanted to make sure Malala and the other girls in his school had every opportunity to succeed.

Pakistani girls attend class at a school in Mingora.

Around this time, Malala noticed poor children digging through the city's garbage. The children were searching for anything they could sell. This saddened her deeply. She felt bad that while she went to school, they had to dig through garbage just so they could pay for a meal. So she convinced her father to give some of them free places in his school. Her life of fighting for others had begun.

Malala wasn't always so generous, though. If a girl scored better on an exam, Malala would become very jealous. And when she suspected a friend of stealing one of her toys, Malala began stealing hers. She kept stealing from her friend until she was caught. Then she tried to lie about it.

Malala had to go and apologize for what she'd done. She was ashamed and scared that her father would think badly of her. She never wanted to disappoint him. So she vowed never to steal or lie again.

When Malala was ten, the Taliban seized control of Swat. She remembers them coming in at night. She said that she thought of them like the evil vampires in the *Twilight* books she was reading.

At first, things didn't change much. The Taliban leader, Maulana Fazlullah, claimed to have come to help the people of Swat follow the Quran, Islam's holy book. He asked for mostly harmless things, such as for men to grow beards.

But in time, the Taliban grew more controlling. Slowly, they were taking away the rights of Swat's people—especially the women. Fazlullah demanded that people stop listening to music and dancing. Soon the Taliban were taking away people's CDs, DVDs, and TVs. They burned down music shops and movie theaters. They banned the recording of films and music, driving artists from the region. Anything that the Taliban felt threatened Islam was at risk. They even destroyed famous statues of Buddha that had stood for centuries.

"All this happened and nobody did a thing," Malala wrote. "It was as though everyone was in a trance."

Standing Opposed

Most people in Swat knew that angering the Taliban could be a death sentence. But Ziauddin was one of a handful of community leaders who did publicly criticize the Taliban. He did not close his schools, even as the class sizes began to drop.

Things continued to get worse. In 2007 the Taliban captured and killed one of Ziauddin's friends. They claimed the man had helped the Americans in the war. Then, in 2008, Fazlullah named Ziauddin an opponent, or enemy, of the Taliban. Ziauddin had to be careful. He knew that the Taliban wanted him dead. He didn't stay in one place long. The family kept a long ladder in their home.

Ziauddin Yousafzai, Malala's father, was named an opponent of the Taliban for his support of educating girls.

Ziauddin could use it to escape if the Taliban ever came for him.

Many of Ziauddin's friends and family begged him to renounce, or take back, the bad things he'd said about the Taliban. If he did, he would be safe. But he refused. He continued to speak out against them. Malala feared for her father's life.

It was a scary time for Malala. She loved school. But she had to hide her books. She couldn't wear her school uniform. She worried that every man she passed on the street would challenge her.

The Taliban bombed this school to rubble because it was used to educate girls.

Then the Taliban began blowing up schools. One in Malala's own town was destroyed in February 2008. By the end of that year, the Taliban had destroyed about four hundred schools in the region.

Ziauddin never backed down. And eleven-year-old Malala decided it was time for her to speak as well. Reporters wanted to talk to young female students, but few were willing to risk it. Malala stepped up. She agreed to several interviews with TV and newspaper reporters. "How dare the Taliban take away my basic right to education?" she demanded on the television station BBC Urdu (Urdu is the main language of Pakistan).

Many people were amazed by Malala's bravery. Few adults dared speak out against the Taliban, even in the safety of their own homes. And here was a child, openly challenging them on television! She was quickly becoming the face of girls' rights in Pakistan. And her role in the struggle was about to get even bigger.

Through the Eyes of a Child

Aamer Ahmed Khan was the editor of the BBC Urdu website. He followed the struggle in Swat carefully. Khan wanted to bring the story to the rest of Pakistan— and to the whole world. But he had an unusual idea about how to do it. He wanted a female student to write

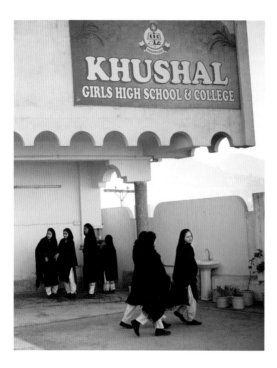

Malala attended Khushal Girls High School and College, which is how Khan got in touch with her about writing a blog.

a blog (a public Internet diary) about what it was like to live in a Taliban-controlled area.

Through a friend, Khan asked Ziauddin to help him find such a student. At first, another girl from Ziauddin's school volunteered. But her family wouldn't let her do it. It was too dangerous, they argued. Malala overheard her father discussing the idea. "Why not me?" she asked.

Ziauddin agreed to let Malala write the blog. But she had to be careful. She used a pen name, Gul Makai. And her contact with the BBC Urdu website never called her from a work phone. He feared that someone could trace the calls and find out who she was. So instead, he used his wife's phone, which no one would think to track.

Malala, by this time a seventh grader, was eager to share her experiences with the world. Her first blog entry, dated January 3, 2009, was titled "I Am Afraid." In it, she revealed how much life had changed since the Taliban had come. She described terrible dreams and the fear she felt just walking down the street.

At first, a writer at the BBC Urdu website helped Malala write and organize her thoughts. But the words were her own. She was only eleven, so much of what she wrote was simple and direct. The fear of a young girl really came through in her writing, and this captured the attention of an ever-growing audience.

Soon people throughout Pakistan and around the world were reading Malala's blog. It was written in the Urdu language, but newspapers everywhere translated

They cannot stop me. I will get my education if it's at home, school or somewhere else. This is our request to the world—to save our schools, save our Pakistan, save our Swat.

—Malala Yousafzai

and printed parts of it. In time, Malala grew more comfortable with the writing. She realized that her words could change the way people thought. It was her way of fighting back, and she was very good at it.

Malala's First Blog Post—"I Am Afraid"

I had a terrible dream yesterday with military helicopters and the Taleban. I have had such dreams since the launch of the military operation in Swat. My mother made me breakfast and I went off to school. I was afraid going to school because the Taleban had issued an edict banning all girls from attending schools.

Only 11 students attended the class out of 27. The number decreased because of Taleban's edict. My three friends have shifted to Peshawar, Lahore, and Rawalpindi with their families after this edict.

On my way from school to home, I heard a man saying 'I will kill you.' I hastened my pace and after a while I looked back if the man was still coming behind me. But to my utter relief, he was talking on his mobile and must have been threatening someone else over the phone.

Malala's blog (*to the right*) was written in the Urdu language, but the BBC also translated it into English.

Early on, Malala almost slipped up several times. Her schoolmates sometimes talked about the blog, but she knew she couldn't tell them that she was Gul Makai. And in one of her blog posts, she accidentally let some information slip. She admitted that her real name meant "grief stricken." A reader could have used that information to figure out her real name. But if anyone did, nothing happened.

By 2009 the Taliban had officially banned the education of girls. Malala wrote about her sadness and frustration at being forced from her beloved school.

The Taliban's official ban began January 15, 2009. The *New York Times* was working on a documentary—titled *Class Dismissed in Swat Valley*—about the school closings. The newspaper sent a reporter and a camera crew to follow Malala to her last day of school before it closed. "They cannot stop me," Malala told the camera. "I will get my education if it's at home, school or somewhere else. This is our request to the world—to save our schools, save our Pakistan, save our Swat."

War Zone

Malala wasn't the only person in Pakistan protesting the ban. By February increasing pressure forced Fazlullah to back off his stance. He agreed that girls under the age of ten could return to classes. Malala was eleven. But like many others her age, she pretended to be younger so she could return to school. She didn't write about this in her blog, however. It was her secret.

During this time, the Taliban and Pakistan's military had been fighting over control of Swat. In late February of 2009, the two sides agreed to a peace deal. As part of the deal, the Taliban gave up control of Swat. Malala was thrilled. She was finally able to go back to school without fear. The editors at the BBC Urdu website decided that Malala's blog had served its purpose. Her last entry was dated March 12.

But the happiness at the peace deal was short-lived. In truth, little changed in Swat. The Taliban remained, and according to Malala, they were more brutal than ever. Soon the Pakistani military and the Taliban were fighting again, and the violence was getting closer. Malala could hear explosions from her home.

By early May, the fighting had grown more intense. Mingora was evacuated. Malala had to pack up her things and go to live with extended family in the countryside.

"Leaving our home felt like having my heart ripped out," she wrote. "I stood on our roof looking at the mountains. . . . Everything was silent, pin-drop silent. There was no sound from the river or the wind. Even the birds were not chirping. I wanted to cry because I felt in my heart I might never see my home again."

It was a difficult time. The family moved from home to home, village to village. Malala's birthday came and went, and nobody even noticed. She was sad and homesick and often bored. But she knew it was far worse for many others. The Yousafzais had family to take them in. Tens of thousands of others were forced to live in refugee camps.

More than two months later, the ordeal ended. Pakistan's army drove the Taliban out of Swat. Malala and her family finally got to go home. She was nervous as they returned. They saw bullet holes in homes, wrecked signs, and buildings destroyed. It hardly looked like the same place. But Malala was relieved to find that her home had not been touched. And the school building had suffered only minor damage.

Our school bell rang again.... It was wonderful to hear that sound and run through the doorway and up the steps as we used to.... We knew we were lucky. Many children had to have their classes in tents because the Taliban had destroyed their schools.

— Malala Yousafzai

By August things were returning to normal. "Our school bell rang again," Malala wrote. "It was wonderful to hear that sound and run through the doorway and up the steps as we used to. I was overjoyed to see all my old friends.... We knew we were lucky. Many children had to have their classes in tents because the Taliban had destroyed their schools."

$\mathcal{G}$rowing Fame, Growing Danger

Malala enjoyed her return home. But she knew that the struggle for girls' rights was far from over. The Taliban was gone. But they still had a big influence on many of its people. Many of these people still wanted to keep girls out of school.

Malala wanted to keep working to change minds. So she continued to do interviews with reporters from around the world. During this time, Malala became interested in journalism. She had always imagined herself as a doctor or a politician. But she had seen the power that good reporting could have. She thought she would like to be a journalist one day.

Malala's fame continued to grow. She remained a powerful voice for girls' rights. In late 2009, she was nominated for an International Peace Prize. It was an honor, but it came at a price—the secret that she had been Gul Makai was out. There was no immediate response from the Taliban. But it was one more reason for the Taliban to be angry with Malala and her father.

The summer of 2010 brought disaster to Pakistan. Heavy monsoon rains pounded the region. The Indus River flooded. Thousands drowned, while millions were left homeless.

To make things worse, the Taliban had cut down many of the trees in the mountains surrounding the Swat Valley. They sold the wood from the trees to make a profit. Normally, the trees would have helped anchor the soil in place. But without them, dirt turned into mud, which flowed down the slopes. Huge mudslides swept into the valley. Malala's school was flooded with water and mud. Many of Swat's bridges were wiped out.

Many Swat Valley homes were damaged when the Indus River flooded in 2010. It was the worst flood in more than eighty years, affecting 20 million people.

Victims of the flood carry relief goods over a damaged bridge in Kallam, a town of Swat Valley.

Swat was cut off from the world. There was no electricity. The drinking water was tainted. Soon, disease began to spread. The situation just seemed to get worse and worse. The Taliban wasted little time in taking advantage of what was going on. Swat was again an easy target. A little more than a year after the Taliban had been driven from Swat, they returned. And once again, Malala's school—and girls' schools throughout the region—were in danger.

As the crisis continued, Malala grew frustrated by the lack of help from the government. Pakistan's president, Asif

Ali Zardari, was on vacation in France during the disaster.

"We felt frustrated and scared once again," Malala later wrote. "I had thought about becoming a politician and now I knew that was the right choice. Our country had so many crises and no real leaders to tackle them."

Malala was, in many ways, already a leader. And around the world, more and more people were noticing. In 2011 South African civil rights activist Desmond Tutu nominated her for the International Children's Peace Prize—a prize awarded each year to a child for his or her commitment to advancing children's rights. She was the first person from Pakistan ever to be nominated.

Desmond Tutu, former South African archbishop, nominated Malala for the International Children's Peace Prize.

"Malala dared to stand up for herself and other girls," Tutu explained. "[She] used national and international media to let the world know girls should also have the right to go to school."

Malala didn't win that award, but other honors followed. In December 2011, Pakistan's prime minister, Yousaf Raza Gillani, awarded her Pakistan's first National Peace Award for Youth (a prize that has since been awarded every year since 2011 and called the Malala Prize). At the ceremony, Malala explained her actions. "In a situation where a lifelong school break was being imposed upon us by the terrorists," she said, "rising up against that became very important, essential."

Pakistan's former prime minister Yousaf Raza Gillani awarded Malala Pakistan's first National Peace Award for Youth, which was later named the Malala Prize.

Even if they come to kill me, I will tell them what they are trying to do is wrong, that education is our basic right.

— *Malala Yousafzai*

Malala was asked about how she would react if the Taliban came for her. "I think of it often and imagine the scene clearly," she answered. "Even if they come to kill me, I will tell them what they are trying to do is wrong, that education is our basic right."

Of course, the Taliban disagreed. "She was pro-West, she was speaking against the Taliban," a Taliban spokesperson later explained. "She was calling President Obama her idol. . . . She was young but she was promoting Western culture in Pashtun areas."

To the Taliban, that was unacceptable. And so they began to make plans to eliminate her.

Shots Fired

Malala had earned a large sum of money with her National Peace Award. She used some of it to help her family. But with the rest, she wanted to start a foundation. She remembered seeing the children scavenging through garbage. Her foundation would work to make sure every child in Pakistan had an equal chance for an education.

In January 2012, Malala learned that the Taliban had issued a death threat against her. Ziauddin suggested that they stop their fight for a time to let things cool down.

If we believe in something greater than our lives, then our voices will only multiply even if we are dead.

— *Malala Yousafzai*

"How can we do that?" Malala answered. "You were the one who said if we believe in something greater than our lives, then our voices will only multiply even if we are dead. We can't disown our campaign."

Malala didn't really take the death threat seriously. She reasoned that the Taliban would never attack a young girl. So she went on speaking and giving interviews. She missed a lot of school during her travels, however, and regretted slipping to second in her class.

Malala celebrated her fourteenth birthday on July 12, 2012. According to Islamic tradition, this meant that she was an adult. Many Islamic girls are married at this age. But Malala's family was in no rush for her to find a husband. They wanted her to live with them and stay in school. Still, while Malala's home life might not have changed, one thing did. In the eyes of the

Taliban, she was no longer a child. The risk to her was greater than ever.

Ziauddin shared the risk. He felt that danger more keenly than ever before. He changed his daily routine so that it would be hard to predict where he'd be.

Meanwhile, Malala had taken her fight to the Internet. She started a Facebook page, which drew both admirers and those who wished to silence her. Her page was often smeared with hateful comments by Taliban sympathizers.

Malala began to take the threats more seriously. Every night, she made sure all the family's doors and

Social Media

Malala quickly learned the power of using social media to get her message out. Her blog generated lots of feedback and comments. But Malala wasn't able to interact directly with the people who commented.

When Malala started a Facebook page, that changed. Through the popular social media site, Malala could communicate directly with people around the world. Her account drew a lot of attention. People were fascinated by the chance to read about her life in Swat. Many sent her encouraging messages.

But there was also a darker side. Taliban supporters often tried to smear her page with hateful messages and threats. Malala tried to ignore the negative posts and focus on the positive.

windows were locked. She prayed to Allah (God) to keep her safe.

Yet her focus remained on school. She was still bothered that she'd finished second in her class the previous spring. She was determined to regain the top spot after the school's week of October exams. On Monday, October 8, Malala took her physics exam. Then she went home to prepare for Tuesday's exam in Pakistan studies. It wasn't her best subject, so she stayed up late studying.

Her hard work paid off. The exam went well, and as Malala climbed aboard the bus with her classmates, she was feeling confident. She was happily singing with her friends when the bus rolled to a stop. Two men came aboard, and one of them shot her.

Critical Condition

The first shot hit Malala in the head, then went into her neck and lodged itself near her spine. The bullet hadn't gone into her brain. But pieces of her skull had. It was a grave injury.

The bus driver reacted quickly. As Moniba held Malala's bleeding head in her lap, the driver sped from the scene and drove to a nearby hospital. From there, Malala was airlifted to a military hospital in nearby Peshawar.

Her condition was critical. Part of her brain was badly swollen. Doctors had to perform emergency surgeries to keep her alive.

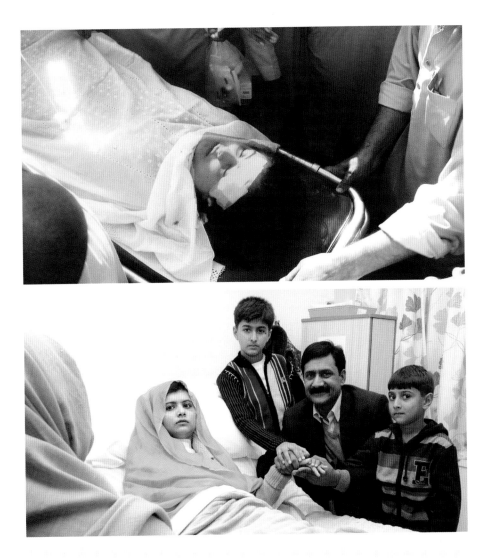

Top: Pakistani hospital workers carry an injured Malala on a stretcher after she was shot by a member of the Taliban. She was shot in the head.

Bottom: Malala sits up in her hospital bed with her father and two brothers, Atal Khan (*left*) and Khushal Khan (*right*), at Queen Elizabeth Hospital Birmingham.

Malala's family, along with a large group of reporters, waited for news. Surgeon Mumtaz Khan addressed the reporters. "Malala is still in critical condition and has been shifted to the intensive care unit of the hospital," he said. "But I am optimistic and by the grace of Allah she will recover."

Malala was still in a coma. Doctors gave her a 70 percent chance to live. She needed a more modern hospital. Offers to treat her came in from around the world. On October 15, six days after the attack, Malala was stable enough to be moved to Queen Elizabeth Hospital Birmingham in England.

Malala spent the next three months in the hospital. She came out of her coma on October 16. She was confused and couldn't talk. She had to communicate with nurses by blinking or pointing at letters on a board. But over time, she got better. She was finally able to leave the hospital on January 3, 2013. Surgeries had helped to rebuild her skull and repair much of the damage that had been done.

Meanwhile, people in Pakistan and around the world were outraged by what had happened to Malala. Huge rallies against the shooting were held in several Pakistan cities. Two million people signed a petition calling for a law to guarantee education rights to all Pakistan's children (the law later passed).

Yet the Taliban refused to back down. They vowed to target Malala again.

Top: Pakistani civil society activists and journalists carry candles and photographs of Malala while she remains in critical condition.

Bottom: Pakistani female students recite verses from the Quran as they pray for Malala's recovery.

The World Stage

Malala's life would never be the same. Pakistan was no longer safe for her. So she and her family moved to England. And Malala had become famous worldwide. Her face was all over the news. Reporters, entertainers, and world leaders all wanted to meet her.

On Malala's sixteenth birthday, she stood before the

United Nations to make her first public speech since the shooting. She wore a white shawl around her shoulders. The garment had once belonged to former

Malala advocates for girls' education at the United Nations Youth Assembly. Her birthday, July 12, was declared Malala Day by the UN.

Benazir Bhutto, the first female prime minister of an Islamic state, is one of Malala's heroes.

Pakistani prime minister Benazir Bhutto, one of Malala's heroes.

"The terrorists thought they would change my aims and stop my ambitions," Malala said. "But nothing changed in my life except this: weakness, fear and hopelessness died. Strength, power and courage was born."

Malala's courage was recognized when she was nominated for the Nobel Peace Prize. Although she didn't win the award, she was the youngest person ever nominated. And she wasn't about to let her growing fame go to waste. She embraced the world stage, traveling all over to spread her message. She even wrote a book about her life. The biography, *I Am Malala*, was released in October 2013.

Malala traveled to the United States that month to promote her book. She met with President Barack Obama and First Lady Michelle Obama. But Malala wasn't just there to receive praise from the Obamas. She also had a message for one of the most powerful people in the world. Malala challenged Obama, calling for him to end drone (unmanned plane) strikes in Pakistan. It was just further proof that nobody was big enough to intimidate this teenager.

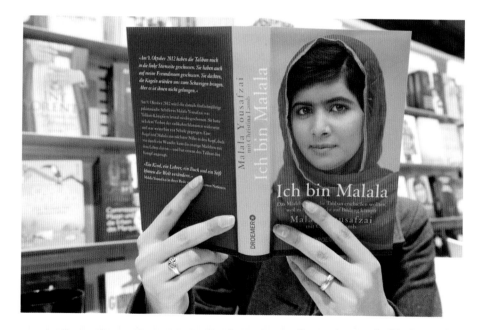

Malala's biography, *I Am Malala*, has been translated into many languages.

Malala meets US president Barack Obama and First Lady Michelle Obama at the White House.

What does Malala's future hold? Will the Taliban make another attempt on her life? Will she ever be able to return home? Nothing is certain. But no matter what happens, Malala has become the voice of girls throughout Pakistan. Some call her a threat. But many more call her a hero.

IMPORTANT DATES

1997   Malala Yousafzai is born on July 12 in Mingora, Pakistan.

2001   On September 11, terrorists closely tied to Afghanistan's Taliban attack the United States. The United States declares war on the Taliban.

2004   Seven-year-old Malala is at the top of her class. Islamic traditionalists try to force her father to close his school, but he refuses.

2008   The Taliban controls the Swat District and destroys about four hundred schools. Eleven-year-old Malala begins publicly speaking out for her right to an education.

2009   Malala begins writing a blog for the BBC Urdu website. Taliban forces battle with Pakistan's military.

2010   Heavy rains cause terrible flooding throughout much of Pakistan.

2011   Malala is given Pakistan's first National Peace Award for Youth.

2012	On October 9, a Taliban assassin boards Malala's school bus and shoots her. Malala is gravely wounded but survives the attack. She recovers in a hospital in England.
2013	Malala releases her autobiography, *I Am Malala*, and is nominated for the Nobel Peace Prize. She travels to the United States and meets with President Barack Obama and First Lady Michelle Obama.

SOURCE NOTES

8   Malala Yousafzai, with Christian Lamb, *I Am Malala: The Girl Who Stood Up for Education and Was Shot by the Taliban* (London: Weidenfeld & Nicolson, 2013), 120.

11   Ibid., 33.

12   Ibid., 19.

14   Ibid., 33.

16   Ibid., 66.

19   Ibid., 74.

20   Ibid., 80.

22   Malala Yousafzai, January 3, 2009 (1 a.m.), "I Am Afraid," Malala Yousafzai Full Diary for BBC (Gul Makai) (blog), October 27, 2012, http://www.malala-yousafzai.com/2012/10/Malala-Diary-for-BBC.html.

23   Yousafzai, *I Am Malala*, 83.

24   Ibid., 90.

25–26   Ibid., 98.

29   Ibid., 103.

30   Wajahat S. Khan, Mushtaq Yusufzai, and Alexander Smith, "For Malala Yousufzai, a Nobel Prize Could Cap a Remarkable Year since Taliban Shooting," *World News*, October 10, 2013, http://worldnews.nbcnews.com/_news/2013/10/10/20898839-for-malala-yousufzai-a-nobel-prize-could-cap-a-remarkable-year-since-taliban-shooting.

30 Basharat Peer, "The Girl Who Wanted to Go to School," *New Yorker*, October 10, 2012, http://www.newyorker.com/online /blogs/newsdesk/2012/10/the-girl-who-wanted-to-go-to-school .html.

31 Ibid.

31 Ibid.

31 Ibid.

32 Yousafzai, *I Am Malala*, 113.

32 Ibid.

36 Mushtaq Yusufzai, "Pakistani Teen Blogger Shot by Taliban 'Critical' after Surgery," *NBC News*, October 10, 2012, http:// worldnews.nbcnews.com/_news/2012/10/10/14332088-pakistani -teen-blogger-shot-by-taliban-critical-after-surgery?lite.

39 Michelle Nichols, "Pakistan's Malala, Shot by Taliban, Takes Educational Plea to U.N.," *Reuters*, July 12, 2013, http://www.reuters.com/article/2013/07/12/us-malala-un -idUSBRE96B0IC20130712.

SELECTED BIBLIOGRAPHY

Ellick, Adam B., and Ifran Ashraf. *Class Dismissed: Malala's Story*. *New York Times*, 2012. Accessed January 7, 2014. http://www.nytimes.com/video/world/asia/100000001835296/class-dismissed.html.

Khan, Wajahat S., Mushtaq Yusufzai, and Alexander Smith. "For Malala Yousufzai, a Nobel Prize Could Cap a Remarkable Year since Taliban Shooting." *World News*, October 10, 2013. http://worldnews.nbcnews.com/_news/2013/10/10/20898839-for-malala-yousufzai-a-nobel-prize-could-cap-a-remarkable-year-since-taliban-shooting.

Peer, Basharat. "The Girl Who Wanted to Go to School." *New Yorker*, October 10, 2012. http://www.newyorker.com/online/blogs/newsdesk/2012/10/the-girl-who-wanted-to-go-to-school.html.

Tohid, Owais. "My Conversations with Malala Yousafzai, the Girl Who Stood Up to the Taliban." *Christian Science Monitor*, October 11, 2012. http://www.csmonitor.com/World/Global-News/2012/1011/My-conversations-with-Malala-Yousafzai-the-girl-who-stood-up-to-the-Taliban-video.

Yousafzai, Malala. With Christian Lamb. *I Am Malala: The Girl Who Stood Up for Education and Was Shot by the Taliban*. London: Weidenfeld & Nicolson, 2013.

FURTHER READING

BOOKS

Donaldson, Madeline. *Pakistan.* Minneapolis: Lerner Publications, 2009.

Gerber, Larry. *The Taliban in Afghanistan.* New York: Rosen, 2011.

Williams, Brian. *The War on Terror.* Mankato, MN: Arcturus, 2011.

WEBSITES

The Malala Fund
> http://www.malalafund.org
> The Malala Fund seeks to secure the right to educations for girls around the world. Check out this site to learn how it works.

Malala Yousafzai: Portrait of the Girl Blogger
> http://www.bbc.co.uk/news/magazine-19899540
> Read Malala's famous blog, translated into English, at the BBC website.

Time for Kids—Pakistan
> http://www.timeforkids.com/destination/pakistan
> Check out this site to learn more about Pakistan, its history, landmarks, and the daily lives of its children.

INDEX